paperblanks®

ANDROID JONES
COLLECTION

Les pratiques spirituelles ancestrales rencontrent l'art numérique moderne dans les œuvres d'Android Jones. Son travail incite à se concentrer sur le potentiel de l'éveil, le pouvoir du troisième œil et les répercussions précoces de l'avenir. À travers des couleurs psychédéliques et ultramodernes, une iconographie orientale et une esthétique de science-fiction, Jones s'appuie sur les traditions immémoriales et celles encore à venir.

Im Werk des Android Jones treffen alte spirituelle Bräuche auf moderne Digitalkunst. Seine Kunst lenkt den Beobachter in Richtung des Erwachens, der Kraft des Dritten Auges und des frühen Echos der Zeit, die vor uns liegt. Jones' psychedelische und doch gleichzeitig hypermoderne Farben und seine Symbolik, die östliche Ikonographie mit Science-Fiction-Ästhetik verbindet, basieren auf alten Traditionen ebenso wie auf zukünftigen.

Le opere di Android Jones, con motivi che mescolano antiche pratiche spirituali e arte digitale, invitano lo spettatore a prendere coscienza del potenziale del risveglio spirituale, del potere del terzo occhio e dei primi riverberi del tempo a venire. Con colori psichedelici e iper moderni, e immagini che mescolano iconografia orientale ed estetica fantascientifica d'avanguardia, Jones è un artista che recupera tradizioni antiche e future.

Las prácticas espirituales ancestrales se unen al arte digital en la obra de Android Jones. Sus imágenes invitan a tomar conciencia del potencial del despertar, el poder del tercer ojo y las primeras reverberaciones del tiempo que tenemos por delante. Jones se inspira en las tradiciones antiguas y en las que están por llegar: sus obras de colores psicodélicos y ultramodernos combinan iconografía oriental y una estética de ciencia ficción.

paperblanks®

ANDROID JONES COLLECTION

Humming Dragon

Ancient spiritual practices meet modern digital art in the work of Android Jones. His art asks the viewer to focus on the potential for awakening, the power of the third eye and the early reverberations of the time that lies before us. With colours both psychedelic and hyper-modern, and imagery combining Eastern iconography with a science fiction aesthetic, Jones is an artist who draws on old traditions and those yet to be born.

ISBN: 978-1-4397-8183-8

MINI FORMAT   176 PAGES   LINED

DESIGNED IN CANADA

Art by Android Jones (www.androidjones.com)
Printed on acid-free sustainable forest paper.
© 2022 Paperblanks Ltd. All rights reserved.
No part of this book may be reproduced without written permission from the publisher. Paperblanks are produced by Paperblanks Ltd. and Paperblanks Journals Ltd. Made in China.
North America 1-800-277-5887
Europe 800-3333-8005
Japan 0120-177-153

paperblanks.com